EYE VIEW
JUNGLE ANIMALS

EYE VIEW
JUNGLE ANIMALS

Catherine Ard

weldonowen

Contents

Welcome to the world of animal vision!

Have you ever wondered what it might be like to see through another creature's eyes? Well, you're about to find out! You'll be introduced to some amazing animals and discover the fascinating ways in which their eyes work to meet their survival needs—to find food, meet a mate, and avoid danger. Once you know the science, you'll take a look through their eyes. Of course, no one really knows what an animal sees . . . but it's fun to imagine, based on what scientists think!
First, let's cover some vision basics by discovering how humans see.

Our eyes are spheres, and the part that we can see is just the front. The colored circle is the iris and the black spot is the pupil.

The human eye

Eyes **detect light** and convert it into signals that the brain can understand. At the back of the eye, in an area called the retina, are two kinds of light-sensitive cells called **photoreceptors**. **Rod cells** work in dim light, picking out the shape of things. They don't recognize colors, so when it's dark, we see in shades of gray. **Cone cells** work in bright light, detecting colors.

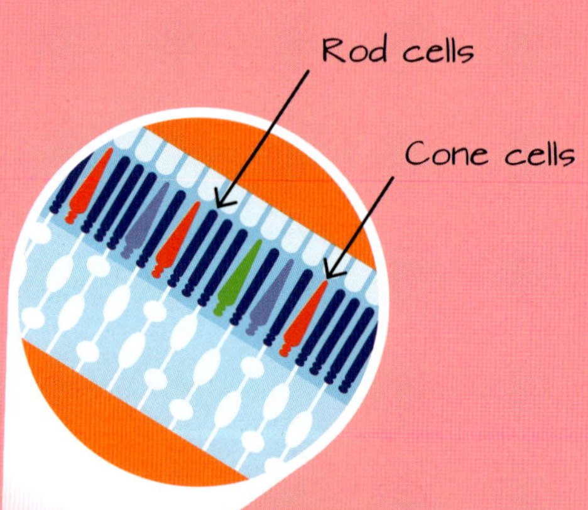

Pupil
The small hole at the center of the iris through which light enters the eye

Lens
The part that focuses light onto the retina

Light ray

Retina
The area at the back of the eye that has light-sensitive cells

Optic nerve
Fibers that carry signals from the retina to the brain

Seeing colors

Light from the sun **looks white**, but it's made up of several different colors. Humans are **trichomats**. This means our cone cells can detect **three colors** of light—red, blue, and green. By combining these, we can see **about a million different shades.**

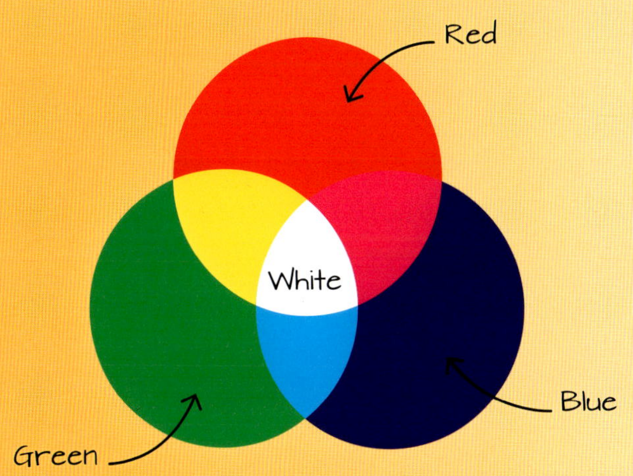

Visible light

Light **travels in waves**. We call the lightwaves the human eye can see "visible light." There are also waves of **infrared and ultraviolet light** that are invisible to us—but not always to an animal.

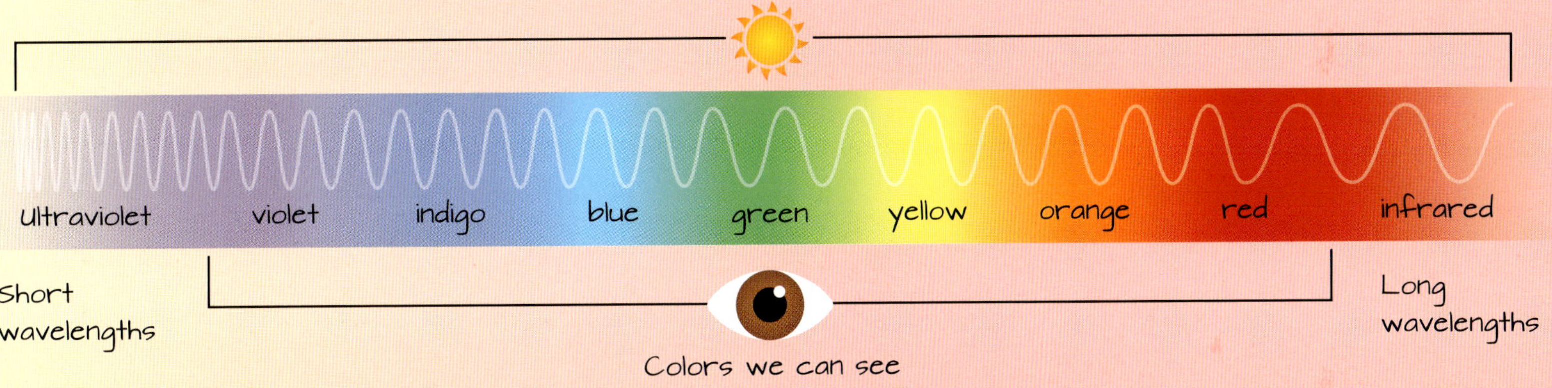

Making sense

The rod and cone cells in your eyes **send information** about the shape and color of the things you see **to the brain** via the **optic nerve**. The brain **sorts out** the information so that you understand what you're seeing.

A banana absorbs all the light spectrum except for yellow. It reflects yellow light into your eyes, so you see a yellow banana.

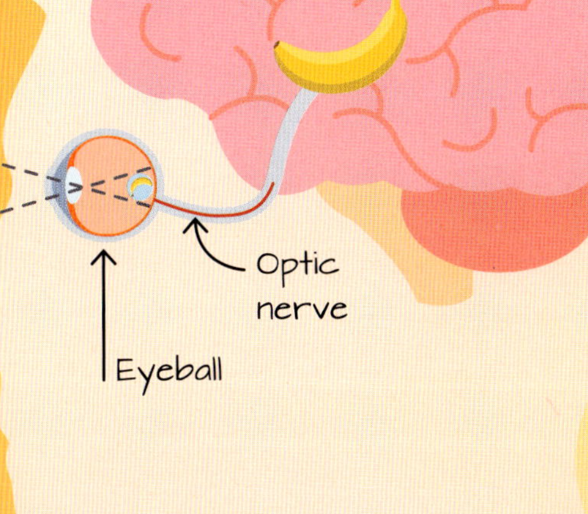

Light is bent by the lens as it enters the eye, which turns the image upside down. The brain decodes this and turns it the right way up.

Near and far

The lens in your eye **changes shape** to focus on objects that are near or far away. To view a **close object**, the eye muscles tighten and the **lens becomes thicker**. This makes the light rays refract, or bend, to focus light on the back of the eye. To view a **distant object**, the muscles relax and the **lens is pulled thinner**. This makes the light bend less.

Eye muscles are the **most active** of all the muscles in the body. They are **100 times stronger** than they need to be for the job they do.

Near vision

Muscles tighten

Distance vision

Muscles relax

Field of vision

Look straight ahead without moving. Everything that you can see is your **field of vision**. Directly in the center of your view is your **binocular vision**—information from both of your eyes that helps you judge distance and see in 3D. Everything you see to the sides is your **peripheral vision**, which is fuzzier and less detailed. What you see above and below your gaze is your **vertical field of vision**.

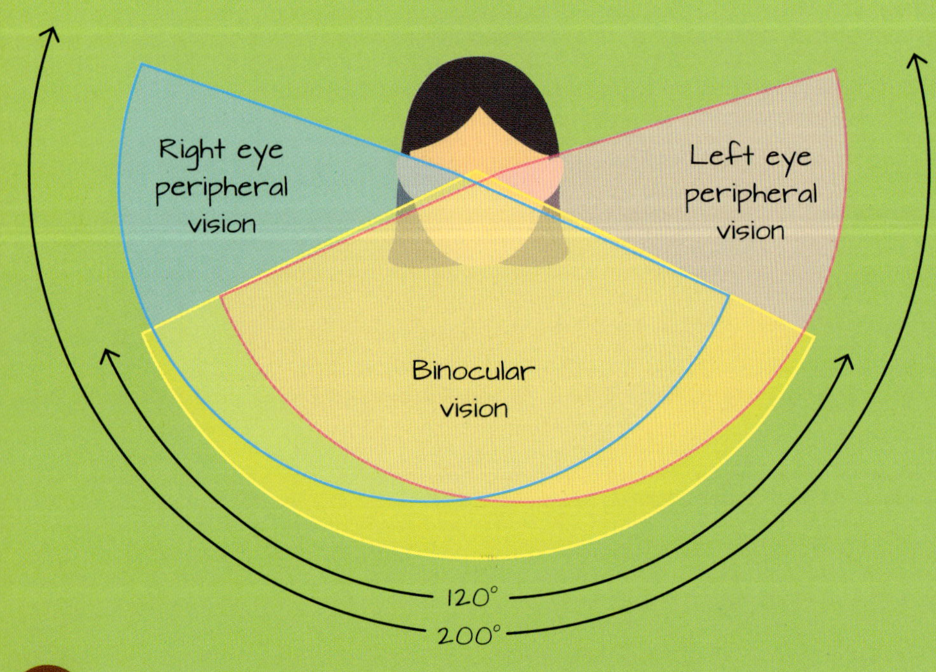

Wild eyes

Every animal's eyes are adapted to suit their environment. The result is a **mind-boggling variety** of eyes in every shape, color, and size. There are peepers as **big as dinner plates** and eyes the size of pinholes. Some creatures have eyes that see colors we can't imagine, while others only see in shades of gray. There are eyes with **thousands of lenses**, eyes that can see underwater, and eyes that see in near-total darkness. There are bulging eyes that **look in opposite directions** at the same time and even eyes with built-in safety goggles.

To discover some **amazing facts** about animal vision, turn the page and **feast your eyes!**

Bengal tiger

Most of the world's Bengal tigers live in the **tropical jungles of India.** These **FUR-ocious** wild cats have sharp **claws,** powerful **jaws,** and **superb eyesight.**

Stealthy stalker

The Bengal tiger prowls through dense forests at dawn and dusk. This stealthy big cat stalks its prey under cover of darkness. It hides in the shadows, spots its victim, and prepares to pounce . . . **It's all over in the blink of an eye.**

Eye View Checklist

- See in the dark ✔
- See underwater
- See in very bright light ✔
- See all around them
- Focus on something in the distance ✔
- Focus on something up close ✔
- Good at detecting movement ✔

Bengal tigers are one of the largest wild cats, with a body length of around six feet and weighing a hefty 450 pounds.

Bright eyes

A tiger's eyes are perfectly adapted for night hunting. They are **packed with rods**—cells that detect movement and shapes in dim light. A shiny layer at the back of the eyes, called the **tapetum lucidum**, bounces light back into the eye, boosting the tiger's sight. The **white fur around the eyes** reflects even more light back into its large pupils.

A tiger can see six times better than a human in the dark!

Killer vision

Like all predators, a tiger has **forward-facing eyes** so it can focus on prey. The views from each eye overlap, giving the tiger **3D binocular vision**. This allows it to judge the distance to its target. The tiger can also **detect movement** at the edge of its vision, thanks to a line of special nerves across the center of its eyes. This helps it to spot other prey and any threats.

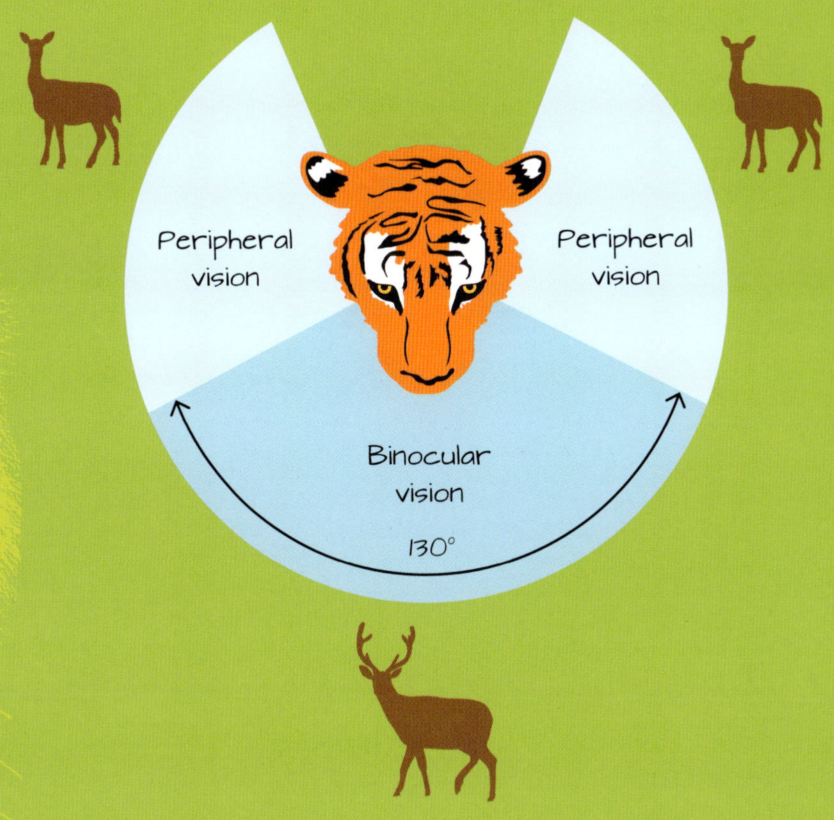

A tiger's stripes are unique— no two animals have the same pattern.

Undercover cat

A tiger's bright orange coat might seem conspicuous to us, but it looks very different through a deer's eyes. Most mammals are **dichromats**. They only have two types of cone cells and can't tell the difference between green and red tones. To a deer, the **tiger blends in** with the green, leafy jungle, with the stripes helping to **break up its outline** among the tall grasses.

Human vision

Deer vision

Now turn the page for an imaginary view of what the tiger sees at night . . .

Our eye view

It's too dark in the jungle for us to see anything. The deer is just a vague shape.

A hungry tiger is on the prowl . . .

. . . and a group of deer prick up their ears, sensing possible danger. They don't spot the tiger lurking in the undergrowth—but it can see them!

The deer can't see the tiger because, to their eyes, its striped coat blends in with the tall grasses.

A tiger's eye view!

Panther chameleon

Using its wandering eyes like a **spy camera,** nothing
escapes the attention of the **panther chameleon.**
It hides in the trees of the Madagascan rainforest,
waiting for **passing prey.**

Crafty chameleon

For most animals, jungle life is a daily battle for survival, but a chameleon has some eye-popping tricks that make life easier. This slow-moving lizard can keep one eye out for danger while the other eye searches for food.

It's almost like it has eyes in the back of its head!

Bulging eyes sit on the sides of the chameleon's head, protected by tough, cone-shaped eyelids that leave just the pupil uncovered.

Eye View Checklist

- See in the dark
- See underwater
- See in very bright light ✔
- See all around them ✔
- Focus on something in the distance
- Focus on something up close ✔
- Good at detecting movement ✔

Seeing double

A chameleon can move each of its eyes independently, so it can look in **two different directions** at once. The eyes stick out from its head, so they can roll around freely, giving a view of **almost 360 degrees**. Because the chameleon can see all around without having to move its body, it doesn't attract attention from predators or prey.

Zoom in

When a chameleon spots its prey, it **brings both eyes together** to focus on its target. The bulging shape of the lens and cornea **magnifies the image**, like a built-in telephoto lens. A small insect could appear as big as a bird to a chameleon's eyes.

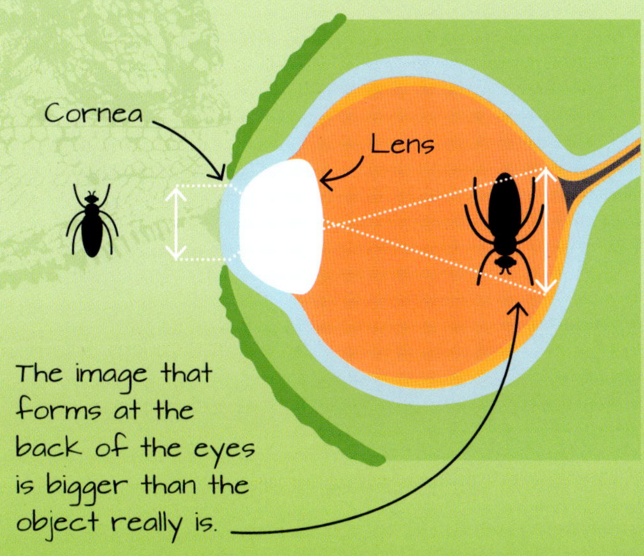

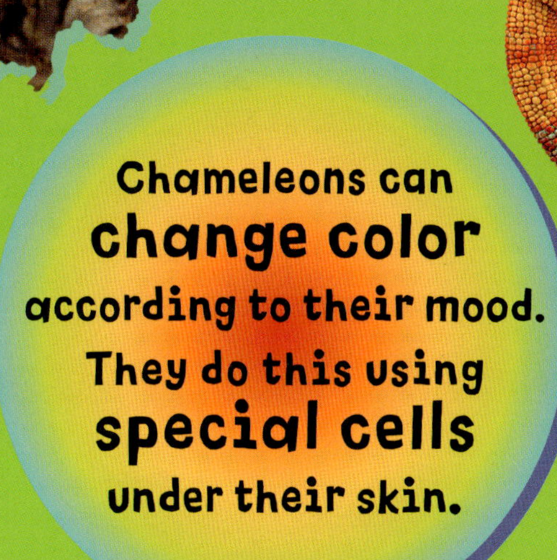

Chameleons can **change color** according to their mood. They do this using **special cells** under their skin.

Killer stare

When it switches to **binocular vision**, with both eyes facing forward, the chameleon sees a **3D image** that allows it to judge how far away an object is with pinpoint accuracy. As soon as prey comes into range, the lizard shoots out its sticky tongue at lightning speed and grabs a snack.

A chameleon's **tongue** can **s t r e t c h** to more than twice its body length.

Now turn the page for an imaginary view of what the chameleon sees in the jungle . . .

Our eye view

At the edges of the scene, our field of vision allows us to see just the snake's head and the lemur's tail.

A chameleon has its eyes on a tasty moon moth for a snack . . .

. . . but the tree boa is also on the lookout for its next meal—a juicy chameleon!

A chameleon's eye view!

Monocular view

The chameleon's eyes can swivel to see much farther around than ours can. Over to the left, there's just a harmless lemur—phew!

Left eye

A chameleon's eye view!

Binocular view

Both eyes together

Right eye

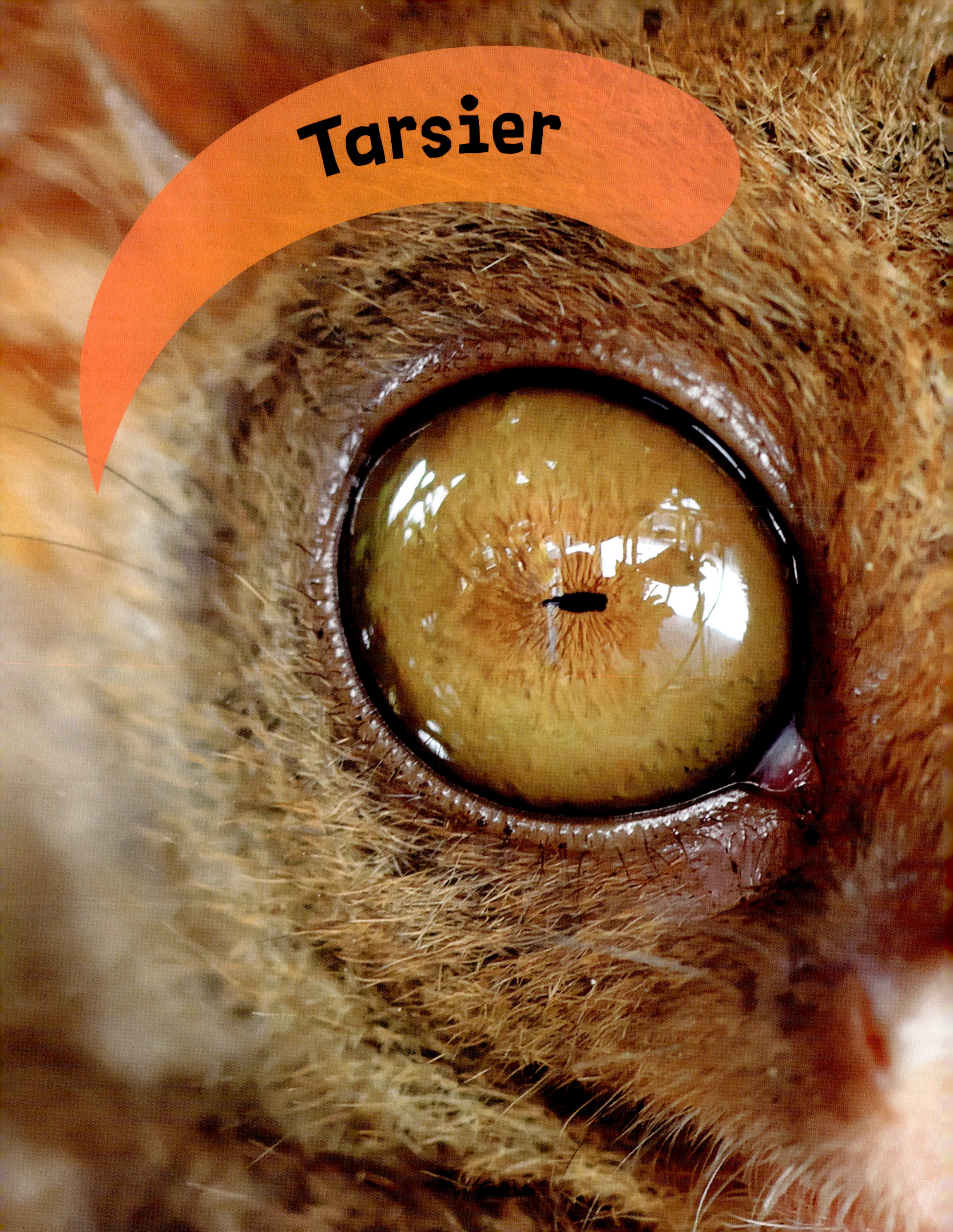
Tarsier

With its **big, round eyes** and furry coat, the tiny tarsier looks super-cute—but don't be fooled. It is a **bug-munching predator** that kills under cover of darkness.

Tiny terror

The tarsier is perfectly suited to see, hear, and hunt in the dark. By day, this little primate can be found dozing on shady branches, but when night falls, the tarsier's special features come into their own. **The tarsier is wide awake, wide-eyed, and ready to spring into action!**

Relative to their body size, tarsiers have the largest eyes of any mammal. Their huge ears pick up the slightest sound.

Eye View Checklist

- See in the dark ✔
- See underwater
- See in very bright light
- See all around them ✔
- Focus on something in the distance
- Focus on something up close
- Good at detecting movement ✔

Giant peepers

Each of the tarsier's eyeballs is **bigger than its brain**. The eyes are too large to swivel in their sockets, but the tarsier has a **flexible neck** that can turn 180 degrees in either direction, just like an owl. This gives it the ability to see more or less **all around** it, while keeping the rest of its body totally still.

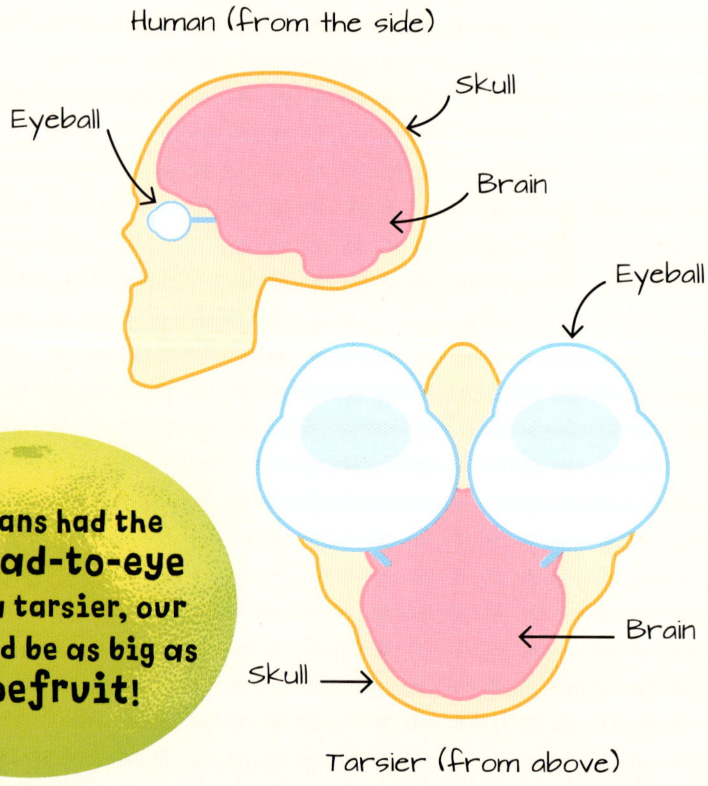

Human (from the side)

Eyeball

Skull

Brain

Eyeball

Brain

Skull

Tarsier (from above)

If humans had the same head-to-eye size as a tarsier, our eyes would be as big as grapefruit!

Night sight

Big eyes help the tarsier to see in the dark. At night, the pupils open into **huge black holes** to let in as much light as possible. At the back of the eye, the tarsier's retina is **packed with rods**—light-sensitive cells that make it possible to see in low light. The rods are so sensitive to light that, during the day, the tarsier's pupils close to **tiny slits** to let in as little bright light as possible.

Eyes at night

Eyes in daylight

Tarsiers are about the size of a **tennis ball** and weigh the same as an **apple.**

Ready and waiting

While hunting, the tarsier sits completely still, watching and listening. Its **huge, swiveling ears** detect the tiny sounds of nearby prey, while its **enormous eyes** pick up every movement. When it's ready, it ambushes unsuspecting insects by leaping up to **ten feet** through the air.

Now turn the page for an imaginary view of how the tarsier sees the forest at night . . .

Our eye view

A human's eyes can't see much in the dark forest.

A young tarsier is on a hunt with his family . . .

. . . His keen eyes spy a tasty katydid on a nearby leaf, but will his sister beat him to it?

Tarsiers' eyes and ears pick up the tiniest movements and sounds made by their insect prey.

A tarsier's eye view!

Crocodile

Look out, there's a crocodile about!
This **ravenous reptile** lurks in steamy swamps,
murky lagoons, and rainforest rivers,
waiting to **snap up** a meaty meal.

Stealth vision

A crocodile waits with its body submerged in the shallow water. Its eyes are perfectly positioned on top of its head to sit just above the surface. This means it can spy on prey at the water's edge without being noticed. **Once its eyes lock on to prey, it prepares to attack . . .**

Eye View Checklist

- See in the dark ✔
- See underwater ✔
- See in very bright light
- See all around them
- Focus on something in the distance ✔
- Focus on something up close
- Good at detecting movement

Wide eyed

Crocodiles can see everything on the shore very clearly because of their specially adapted eyes. The **fovea** is an area on the retina packed with photoreceptors that bring things into **sharp focus**. Your fovea is helping you to see the words on this page right now. A crocodile's fovea is a **long strip**. This allows it to see a wide panorama in detail without having to move its head.

Thick, scaly eyelids guard the crocodile's eyes. During an attack, crocs can draw their eyeballs back into their sockets for extra protection.

Eye protection

Crocodiles have an extra, see-through eyelid called a **nictitating membrane**. Like a set of protective goggles, these close when the crocodile **goes underwater** or when it attacks prey. Crocs can still see underwater but not nearly as well as they can in the open air.

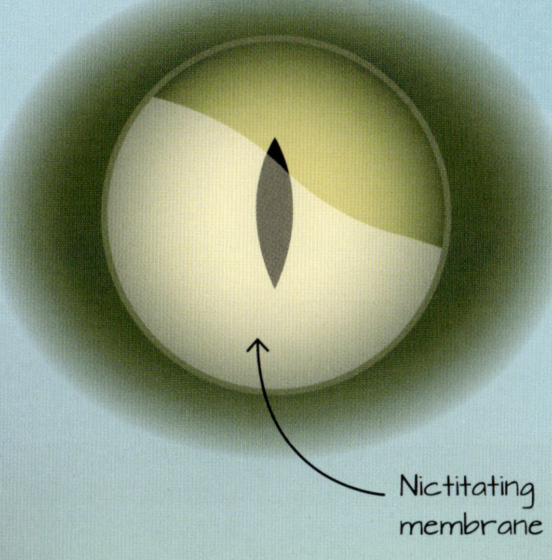

Glow in the dark

Crocodiles have excellent night vision thanks to a layer of mirrorlike cells at the back of the eye called the **tapetum lucidum**. This **reflects light** back into the eye, boosting their vision. Many nocturnal animals have this—it's what makes their eyes shine when you point a torch at them. Crocodile eyes glow a fiery orange.

Crocodiles often sleep with one eye open because only half of their brain sleeps at one time. The other half stays awake and on the lookout.

Researchers in Australia check crocodile numbers by shining bright lights across the water, then counting the pairs of glowing eyes.

Now turn the page for an imaginary view of what the crocodile sees from the swamp . . .

Our eye view

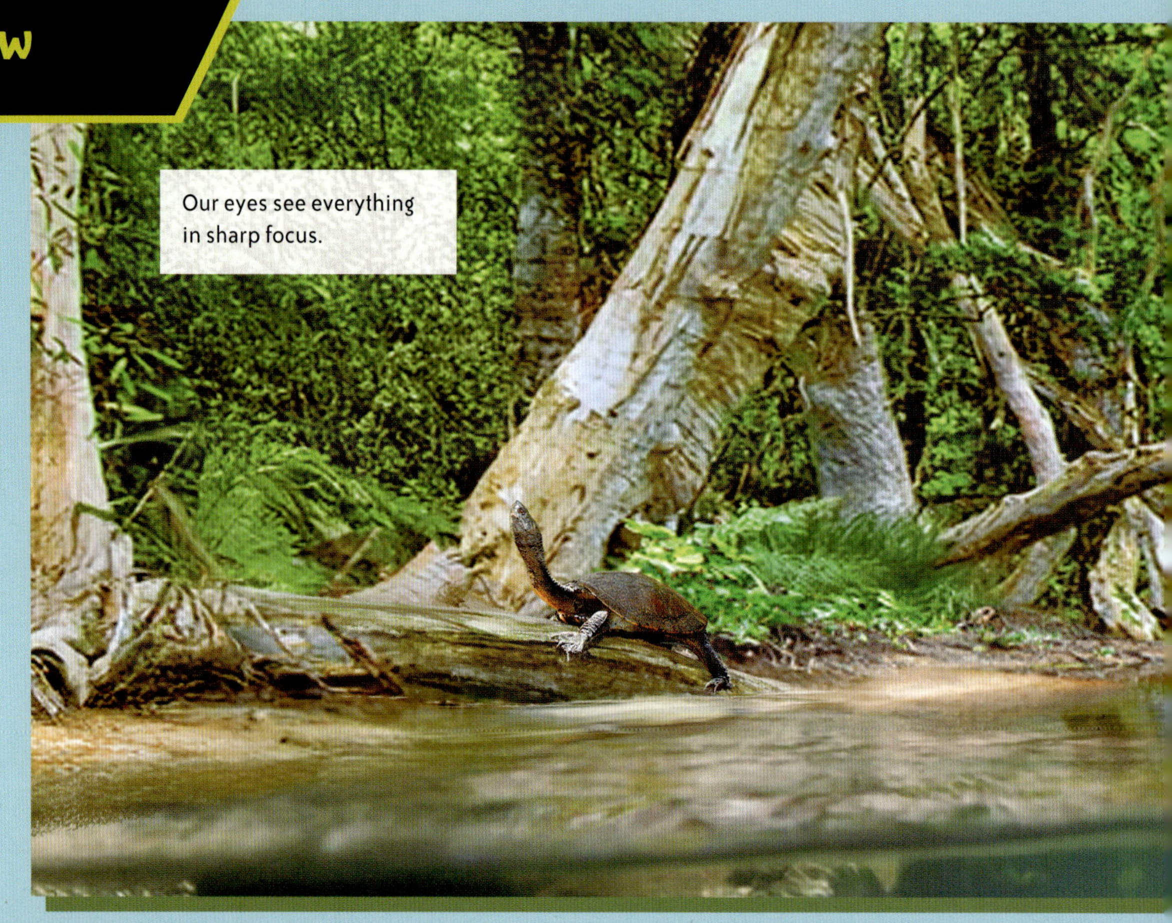

A crocodile is hoping to snap up a bite to eat . . .

. . . and two of its favorite foods are sitting on the shoreline, blissfully unaware of the danger lurking in the swamp.

Our eyes see everything in sharp focus.

A crocodile's eye view!

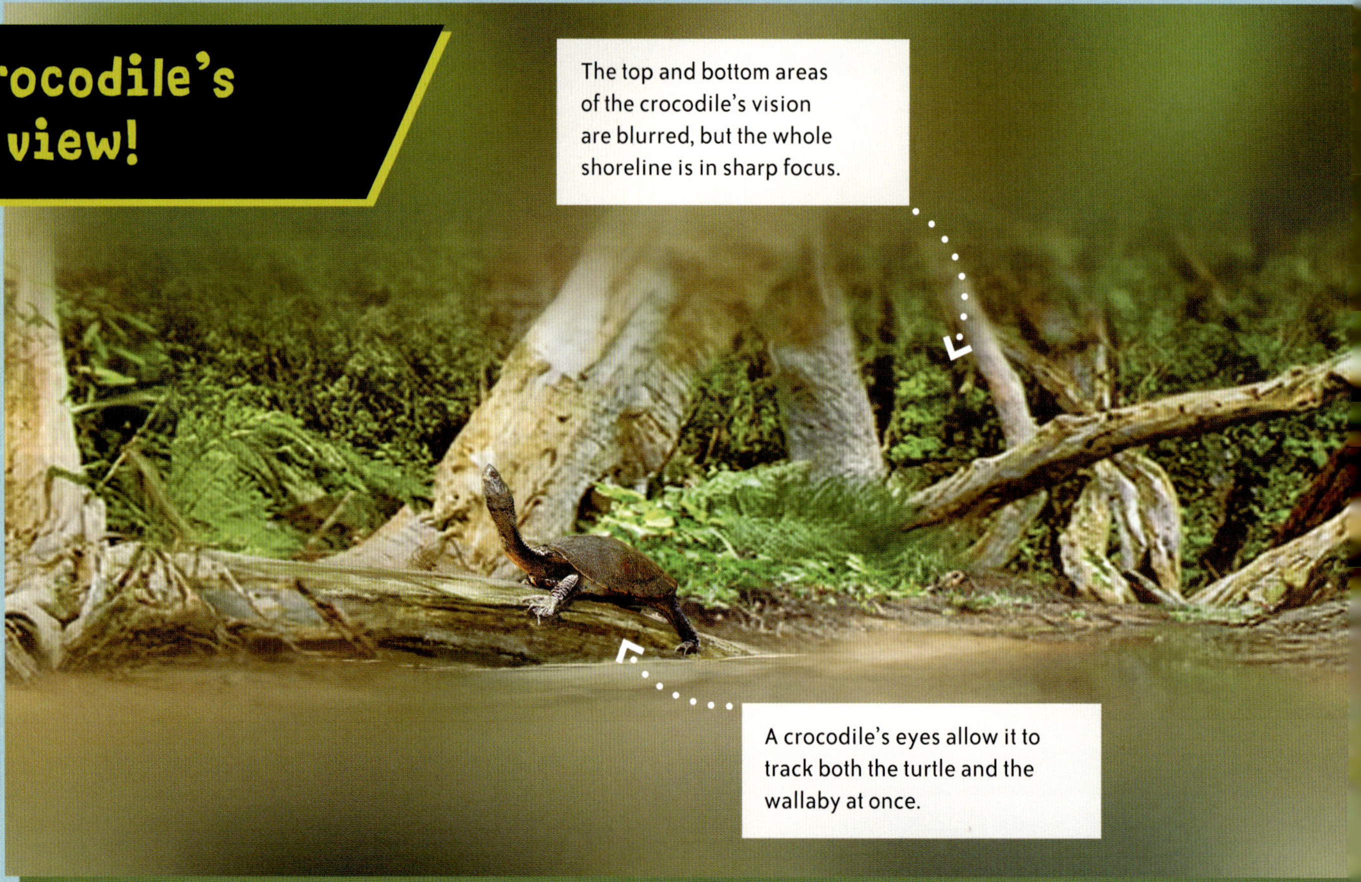
The top and bottom areas of the crocodile's vision are blurred, but the whole shoreline is in sharp focus.
A crocodile's eyes allow it to track both the turtle and the wallaby at once.

The wallaby and the turtle don't know the crocodile is stalking them, as it's almost completely submerged.

Hummingbird

Hummingbirds live in the **Americas.**
These thumb-sized birds are known for their beautiful
colors and **busy, beating wings.**
But these are not their only amazing features . . .

Brilliant bird

The Central and South American rainforests buzz with hummingbirds hovering by crimson flowers. Their dazzling feathers flash with shimmering blues and greens—at least that's what we see... **But hummingbirds can see colors that are totally invisible to us!**

When they dive, hummingbirds flap their wings up to **200 times** per second.

Amazing Technicolor

Humans have three types of color-sensitive cone cells—red, blue, and green. By working together, they allow us to see all the colors of the rainbow and many more. A hummingbird's eyes create colors in the same way, but they have **four types of cone cells**—red, blue, green, and ultraviolet. This mega-mix means their eyes see a Technicolor world that we can't even imagine!

Human color view

Hummingbird color view

Hummingbirds are named after the noise their tiny wings make in flight. They flap so fast that the wings look completely blurred to the human eye.

Eye View Checklist

- See in the dark
- See underwater
- See in very bright light ✔
- See all around them
- Focus on something in the distance ✔
- Focus on something up close ✔
- Good at detecting movement ✔

Flashy colors

A male hummingbird is often more colorful than the female. He uses his radiant feathers to catch her eye. She is looking for a male with **glossy feathers**, as this shows he is healthy. The male's bright colors also help him to **defend his territory**. He flashes his rainbow plumage to show rival males that he means business.

Hummingbirds can hold their position in the air because they make a figure-eight pattern with their wings.

Hummingbirds can fly sideways, backward, and even upside down! This allows them to get into exactly the right position to feed at a flower.

Fast focus

Hummingbirds love to drink flower nectar, but they also snack on insects. Lots of tiny muscles in their eyes mean they can **quickly focus** and **follow speeding objects** much better than a human can. This enables them to **snap flying bugs** straight out of the air, just as if they were moving in slow motion.

Now turn the page for an imaginary view of what the hummingbird sees as it flies through the rainforest . . .

Our eye view

This fly is moving too fast for a human's eyes and brain to process, so we see a blur.

The hummingbird can see the fly clearly because its eyes process information more quickly than ours do.

A hummingbird zooms through the forest . . .

. . . picking out red flowers to feed from. It also spots tasty insects to snap up as they buzz past.

A hummingbird's eye view!

A hummingbird has more peripheral vision than a human, so it can see this toucan perched on a branch.

To a hummingbird, the rainforest glows with unimaginable colors. It is attracted to red, pink, and orange flowers, which many nectar-loving insects can't see.

Red-eyed tree frog

This eye-popping frog lives in rainforest trees.
Its bright-red peepers are its secret weapon
against predators and prey.

Bright-eyed hunter

By day, the red-eyed tree frog hides among the green leaves of the Mexican jungle. By night, it is a top predator, on the lookout for juicy insects. Even though it is almost pitch dark, the frog doesn't miss a single movement.

But the tree frog has some special tricks to make sure it stays safe . . .

Eye View Checklist

- See in the dark ✔
- See underwater ✔
- See in very bright light
- See all around them ✔
- Focus on something in the distance ✔
- Focus on something up close
- Good at detecting movement ✔

The red-eyed tree frog's bright colors are part of its defence. A quick flash of its red eyes, blue body, and orange feet will startle a predator, giving the frog time to leap out of harm's way.

Looking up

A frog's eyes bulge out from the top of its head, giving it a nearly 360-degree view. Most of its vision is **angled upward**. This is handy when it's sitting down at the water's edge, as it can spot predators that are **above and behind it**.

The frog's rear peripheral vision is angled upward.

Eye spy

During the day, the frog **rests under a leaf**. It tucks its bright toes away so that its green skin blends in. Its red eyes are hidden behind a camouflaged eyelid called a **nictitating membrane**. But the frog is **not fully asleep**—the see-through eyelid means it can still be on the lookout for danger.

All change

When a frog begins life as a **tadpole**, its eyes are specially adapted to see underwater. The eyes also sit on the **side of the head** to give a view of approaching danger—tadpoles are a snack for many pond predators. As the tadpole **changes into a frog**, the position of its eyes changes, too. They **move up and bulge out** to better spot prey.

When a frog swallows, it pulls its bulging eyes down into the roof of its mouth to help push the food down its throat!

Side-facing eyes for spotting predators in water

Eyes adapted for life on land

Now turn the page for an imaginary view of how the tree frog sees its rainforest world at night . . .

Our eye view

From its spot high up on a branch, a tree frog scans the rainforest for food . . .

. . . There are plenty of creatures moving about in the darkness—but they are not all on the menu!

A tree frog's eye view!

Scientists think the red-eyed tree frog can see some color in the darkness.

The margay and the spotted paca at the waterhole are clearly visible, thanks to the frog's excellent night vision.

As well as hunting for food, the frog keeps an eye out for predators, such as this spider.

Asian vine snake

Perfectly disguised among rainforest vines,
this Southeast Asian snake remains
virtually invisible to prey—
but its sharp eyes s-s-s-s-see everything!

Stealthy snake

An Asian vine snake slithers silently along a branch, scanning the leafy jungle for lunch. When it spots a tasty little lizard, it locks it in its sights and prepares to strike. You can learn a lot about this stealthy snake by studying its unusual eyes...
Just don't look too closely!

Eye View Checklist

- See in the dark
- See underwater
- See in very bright light ✔
- See all around them
- Focus on something in the distance
- Focus on something up close ✔
- Good at detecting movement ✔

The Asian vine snake can grow to six feet long. Its slender, agile body and lightning speed give it its other name—the Oriental whip snake.

Clever pupils

Snakes with **round pupils** often track down prey during daylight. Round pupils give good all-around vision for hunting on the ground. Snakes with **vertical slit pupils** often hunt at night. Vertical slits limit the amount of vertical detail, such as blades of grass, and help snakes spot prey moving horizontally across the ground. The vine snake has rare, **keyhole-shaped, horizontal slit pupils**. These allow the snake to focus on objects that are moving up or down, such as lizards on tree trunks!

Groovy vision

The vine snake has the **widest binocular vision** of any snake, which makes it a great judge of distance. It has **grooves** that run from its eyes to the tip of its long, pointed snout. These work like **target markers**, helping the snake to **aim its gaze** at its prey.

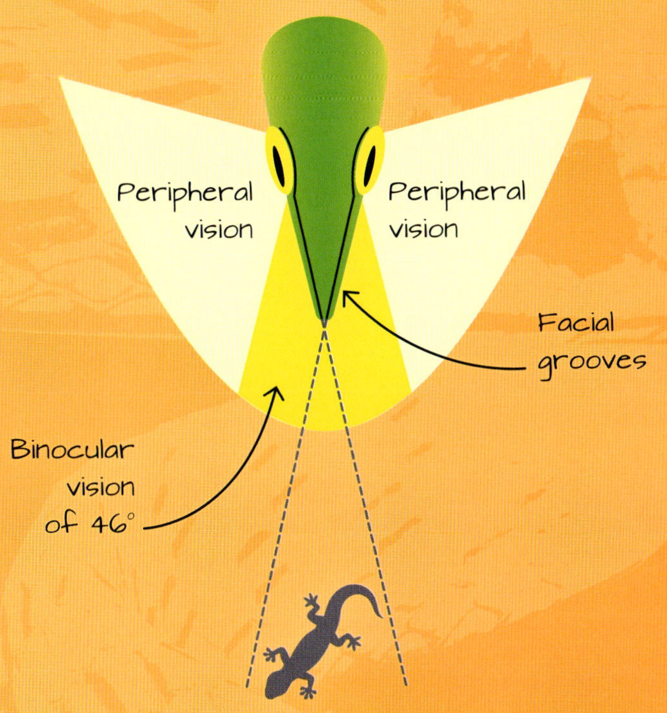

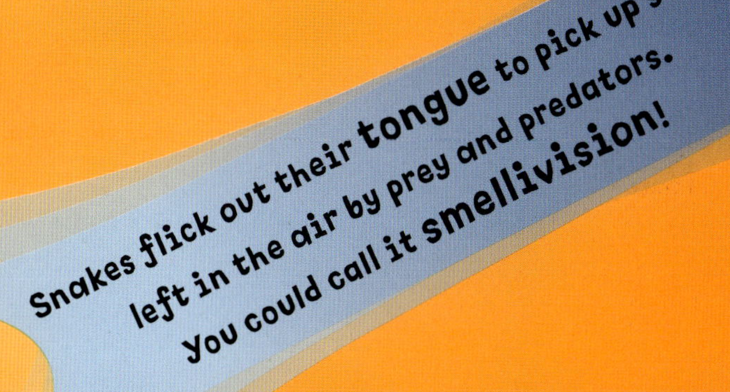

See-through scales

With **no visible eyelids**, a snake's eyes look as if they are always open, even when it's asleep. In fact, it's more accurate to say the eyes are **always closed**, because they are covered with a protective, transparent layer of skin called a **spectacle**, or **brille**. You can see this more clearly when the snake sheds its scaly skin.

Secret shades

Like most snakes that hunt in daylight, the vine snake has **built-in sunglasses**. Yellow-tinted lenses in its eyes protect them from the sun's harmful ultraviolet rays. Scientists also think the yellow tint makes their vision **sharper in bright light**, like ski goggles that block glaring light.

Now turn the page for an imaginary view of what the Asian vine snake sees when it's hunting at the forest's edge . . .

Our eye view

We see less of the jungle, but our vision is more in focus than the snake's.

While a flying frog minds its own business on a leaf . . .

. . . a baby monitor lizard scurries up a tree trunk, hoping to escape the deadly sightlines of the Asian vine snake.

The snake sees blue and yellow colors through protective yellow lenses that shield the sun's harmful rays.

The vine snake's eye view!

Horizontal pupils cut out lots of other detail so that the snake can focus on the vertical movement of the lizard.
The vine snake has a wider field of vision than we have. Without moving its head, it can see an orchid mantis to its right.
By staying still, the flying frog escapes the attention of the snake.

Spectacled owl

The spectacled owl lives in the Amazon rainforest.
Its SPECTAC-ular vision makes it one of the
jungle's most fearsome predators.

Awesome owl

The Amazon rainforest is home to many birds of prey, but after sunset, the spectacled owl rules the roost. This nighttime hunter has many amazing features to help it track down its next meal. **But its superpower is its eyes.**

Eye View Checklist

- See in the dark ✔
- See underwater
- See in very bright light
- See all around them
- Focus on something in the distance ✔
- Focus on something up close
- Good at detecting movement ✔

Owls have the most **forward-facing** eyes of any bird. This makes them **Number 1** for depth perception.

The spectacled owl gets its name from the white bands of feathers around its eyes, which look like a pair of glasses. The eyes face forward, resulting in that famous wise owl stare.

Super focus

The owl's front-facing eyes mean that it doesn't have a wide view of its surroundings, but it does have **3D binocular vision**. Seeing in three dimensions—height, width, and depth—allows it to **judge distances** and pinpoint its prey with deadly precision.

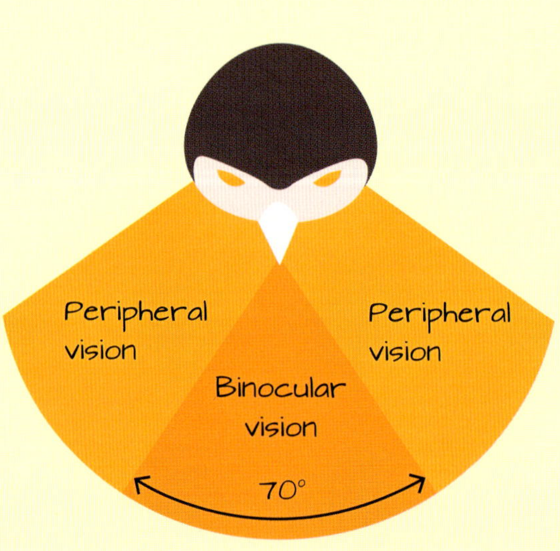

Big eyes, small head

An owl's eyes are huge relative to its head. In order to fit into the bird's tiny skull, the eyes are **tube shaped** rather than spherical. This means the owl **can't roll or move its eyes**—it can only look straight ahead. It makes up for this with its ability to **turn its head around** an amazing 270 degrees!

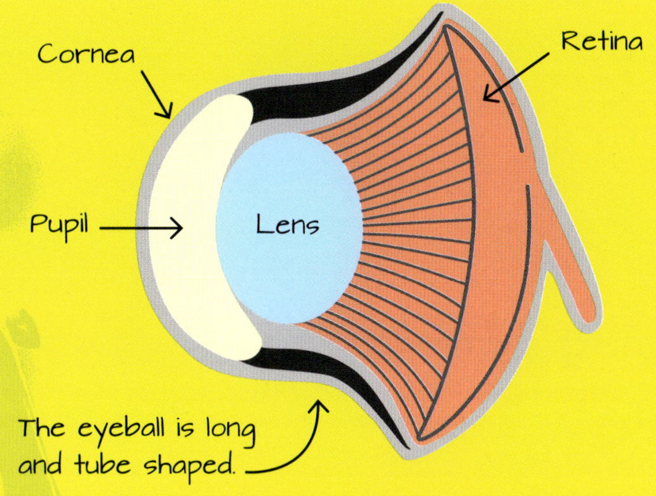

Night watch

Because the spectacled owl is **active at night**, its eyes must be really good at collecting light. The cornea and pupil are big so that **as much light as possible** can enter the eye. The large retina contains lots of **light-sensitive rod cells**, but hardly any cone cells—about 30 rods to every cone. This makes the owl excellent at detecting a scurrying rat from 50 yards away in the dark but not very good at seeing colors.

An owl's eyes are so big that it's possible to see the back of its eyeball when you look down its ear!

Now turn the page for an imaginary view of what the owl sees when it's hunting at night...

Our eye view

A spectacled owl surveys the gloomy forest from its perch . . .

. . . A tree frog and an Amazon bamboo rat are searching for food, but if they don't look out, they could become the owl's dinner!

A spectacled owl's eye view!

The owl's field of vision is narrower than a human's, so it can see less at the edges of the scene.

Large pupils allow the owl to see the forest almost three times as brightly as a human can.

While barely visible to a human, more distant prey, such as the rat, can be easily spotted by the owl.

Ogre-faced spider

If you're wondering how this spider got its name, the answer is **staring you** in the face! These **monster eyes** keep watch all night for a passing meal.

Net trapper

The ogre-faced spider lies in wait at night in the gardens and forests of America, Africa, and Australia, ready to deploy its sticky net trap. **Lightning-fast reactions and enormous eyes make this creepy crawler a lethal bug-catching machine.**

Eye View Checklist

- See in the dark ✔
- See underwater
- See in very bright light
- See all around them ✔
- Focus on something in the distance
- Focus on something up close ✔
- Good at detecting movement ✔

Night light

Like other spiders, the ogre-faced spider has eyes positioned all around its head. At night, its **two huge, forward-facing eyes** allow moonlight to flood in. This light is boosted by a **layer of light-sensitive skin**. The special layer uses a lot of **valuable energy**, so it is destroyed in the bright light of morning when it is no longer needed and **regrows every night** so that the spider can hunt again.

The spindly ogre-faced spider could fit in the palm of your hand. It has the largest eyes of any spider, giving it some of the best night vision on Earth.

> This spider can see **200 times** better at night than a human.

Handy net

When night falls, the spider spins its silk into a **sticky net** about the size of a postage stamp. It spreads the net between its four front legs and **hangs down** from a thread, patiently waiting for passing prey. The net can **stretch up to five times** its original size.

Poop to scoop

To help it trap prey, the ogre-faced spider often drips a few white droppings onto a leaf below its net. These **bright spots of poop** are the **spider's target**. It focuses its huge eyes on the area and becomes motionless. The moment an insect **walks over the spots**, the spider scoops it up in its net.

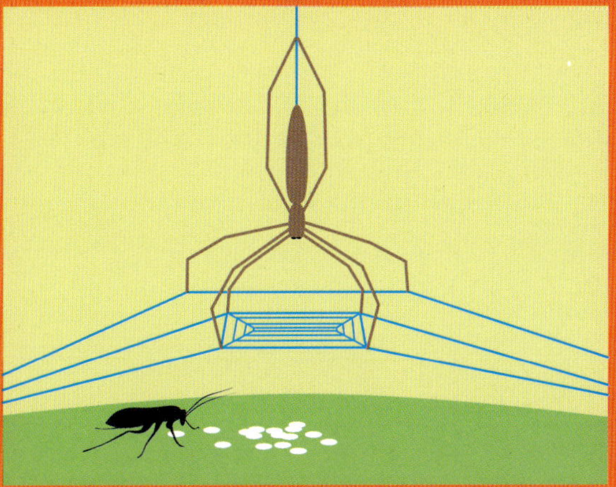

An insect walks toward the target, not knowing the spider is hanging above.

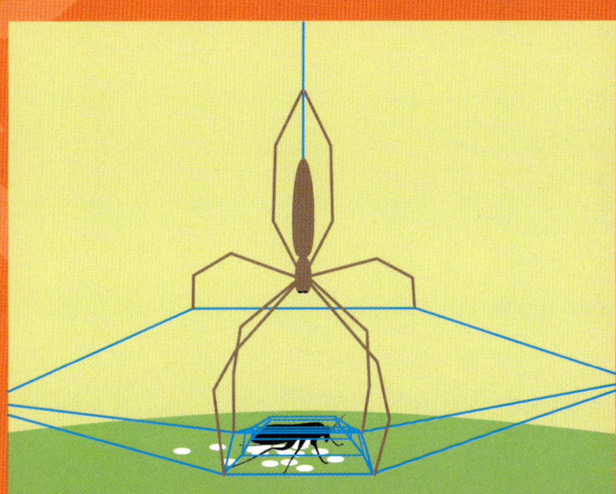

The spider easily spots the insect and captures it in its net.

> To catch flying prey, the ogre-faced spider does a **ninja-style backflip** to trap them in its net.

Now turn the page for an imaginary view of what the ogre-faced spider sees as it hunts in the forest at night...

Our eye view

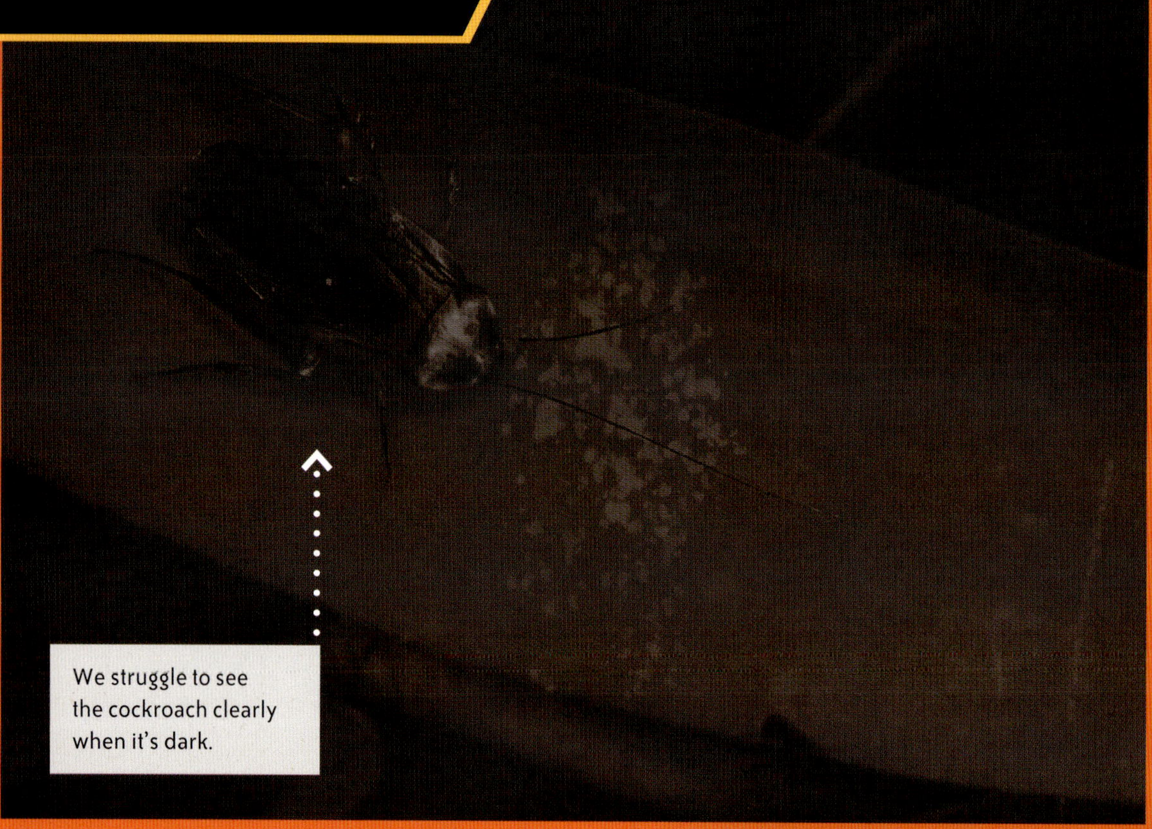

We struggle to see the cockroach clearly when it's dark.

The ogre-faced spider stays perfectly still . . .

. . . for hours on end, watching and waiting. As a cockroach moves into the target area, the spider gets ready to take aim.

The spider's amazing night vision means it can see everything clearly—including its own legs!

An ogre-faced spider's eye view!

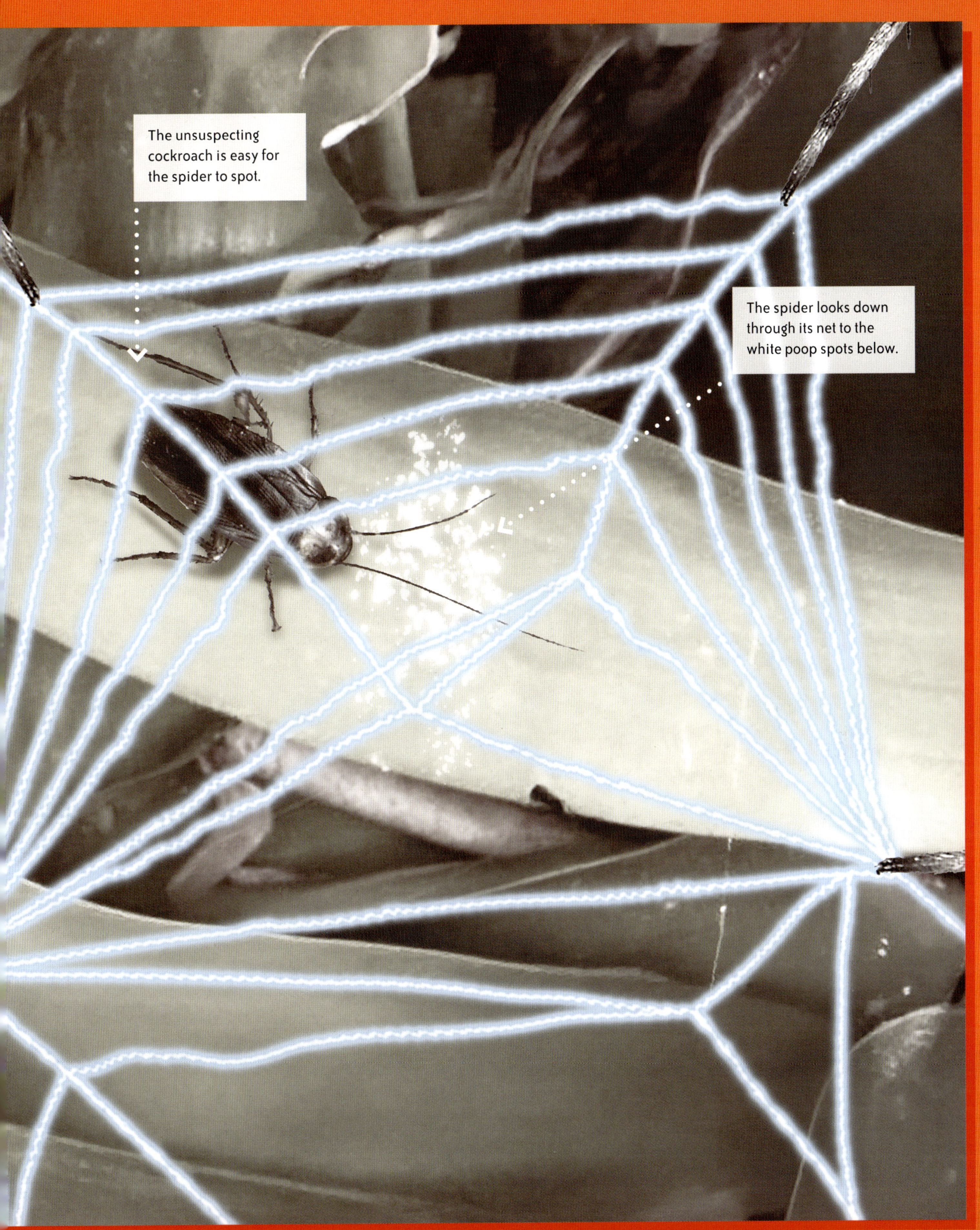
The unsuspecting cockroach is easy for the spider to spot.
The spider looks down through its net to the white poop spots below.

Common bluebottle butterfly

The beautiful common bluebottle butterfly
lives in the **lush rainforests** of Asia.
It has a **secret superpower**—
it sees a hidden world of sparkling colors and patterns.

Color detector

A common bluebottle butterfly flits around the dense Asian rainforest. Our eyes would see an ocean of green, but this butterfly sees a kaleidoscope of glowing shades and patterns. Tropical butterflies have better color vision than most—**but the common bluebottle butterfly takes this to another level.**

Eye View Checklist

- See in the dark
- See underwater
- See in very bright light ✔
- See all around them ✔
- Focus on something in the distance
- Focus on something up close
- Good at detecting movement ✔

This butterfly's caterpillar has six tiny eyes on either side of its head. They can detect light and dark and not much else.

Most butterflies have excellent color vision. They rely on it to select their favorite flowers, find a mate, and spot predators.

Super vision

The common bluebottle butterfly has **15 different types** of **photoreceptor cells**—more than any other insect. Scientists doubt that the butterfly uses *all* its photoreceptors for color vision, but it may mean the butterfly can **see many more shades** than we can and can tell the difference between **colors that look identical to us**.

Human photoreceptors

Three types of photoreceptors combine so that we see millions of colors.

Butterfly photoreceptors

More receptors could mean the butterfly sees a wider range of light wavelengths.

In UV light, **lines and patterns** are revealed on flower petals. They are like **signposts** that lead butterflies to the nectar.

Hidden patterns

Many butterflies **see patterns** that are invisible to the human eye. This is because their eyes detect two kinds of light that we can't see—**ultraviolet and polarized**. In polarized light, glowing wing patterns help butterflies **identify others** of their own species—a crucial part of trying to find a mate! The two species below look **almost the same** to us, but a butterfly would easily be able to **tell them apart**.

Sapho longwing butterfly

Cydno longwing butterfly

All-seeing eyes

Butterflies have **two types of eyes**—simple and compound. The small, simple eyes, called **ocelli**, sense light and movement. The large, compound eyes sense color, brightness, movement, and shape. They are made up of thousands of hexagons, called **facets**. Under each facet is a lens and light-detecting photoreceptor cells. The result is a **wraparound, pixelated view** of the world.

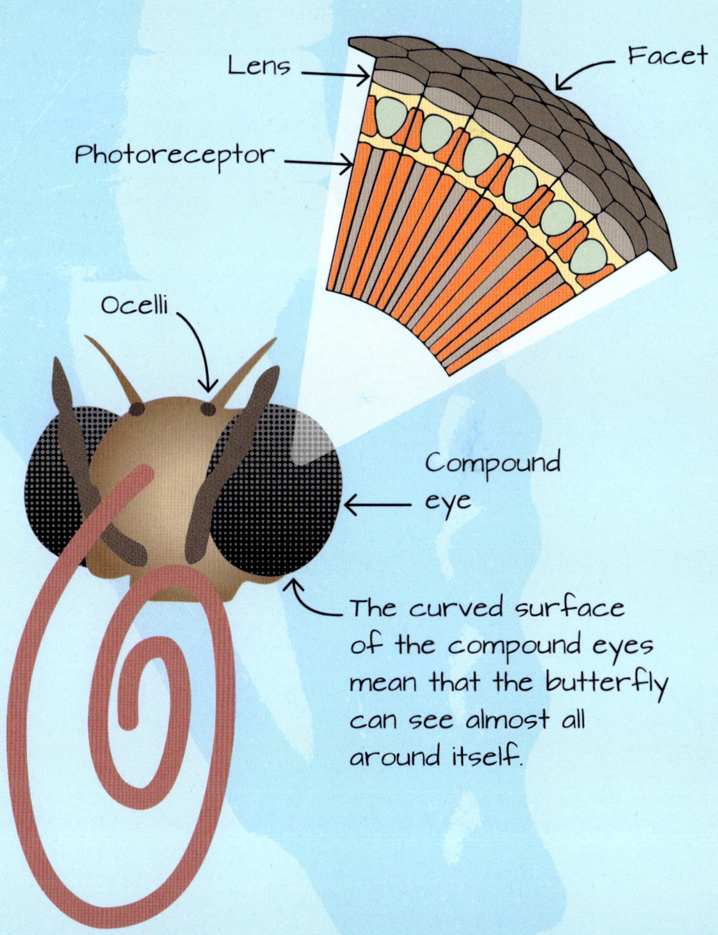

Now turn the page for an imaginary view of how the butterfly sees the forest and other creatures in it . . .

Our eye view

Our field of vision is narrower than the butterfly's, so we see much less of the jungle.

The bluebottle butterfly is trying to find some nectar to eat . . .

. . . but it has a competitor—a black-and-white mime butterfly. It also spots another of its own kind. Could this be a mate?

The butterfly needs to make sure it doesn't get caught in the spider's sticky web.

A common bluebottle butterfly's eye view!

The patterns on this butterfly's wings show it's the right species to be a mate.

Thousands of individual lenses in each eye make a mosaic effect.
Butterflies can see almost all around them—above, below, and to the sides.
A rhinoceros beetle won't harm the butterfly, but it might want some of the same nectar!
UV and polarized light bring out colors and patterns in the jungle that we can't see.

Glossary

360-degree vision—the ability to see all around in a full circle

3D—stands for "three dimensions": length, width, and depth. 3D vision makes objects look solid and enables **depth perception**. See also **binocular vision**.

binocular vision—seeing with both eyes at once. The brain combines the views from each eye to create a single **3D** image. Humans and animals with forward-facing eyes have binocular vision.

compound eyes—eyes with many hundreds or thousands of **facets**, each containing a **lens** and **photoreceptors**. Insects and crustaceans such as crabs, lobsters, and shrimp have compound eyes.

cone cells—the **photoreceptors** in **vertebrates** responsible for color vision in bright light

cornea—a clear dome covering the front part of the eye

depth perception—the ability to judge how far away things are

dichromat—having two types of **cone cell** that are sensitive to two different **wavelengths** of light

facet—one part of a many-sided object. **Compound eyes** are made up of facets.

field of vision—the total area that can be seen when the eyes are fixed in one position

focus—seeing clear, sharp images

fovea—a small hollow in the **retina** that is packed with **photoreceptor** cells. It provides the sharpest vision.

infrared—light with a longer **wavelength** than humans can see. Infrared is visible to some animals.

invertebrate—an animal without a backbone, or spine. See also **vertebrate**.

lens—the part of the eye behind the **pupil** that focuses, or directs, light on to the **retina** to give clear vision

light wave—the way light travels, a bit like ripples in water. S-shaped waves of light from the Sun travel to Earth at different angles.

monocular vision—seeing with one eye at a time. Animals with eyes on either side of their head have monocular vision.

nictitating membrane—a see-through eyelid that is drawn across the eye from the side to protect it. Birds, reptiles, and some mammals have nictitating membranes.

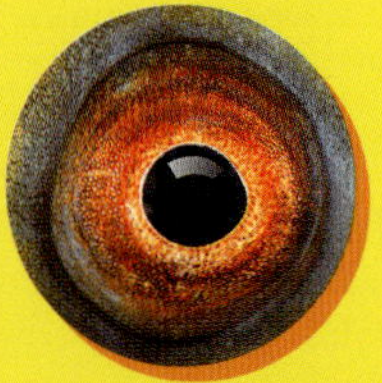    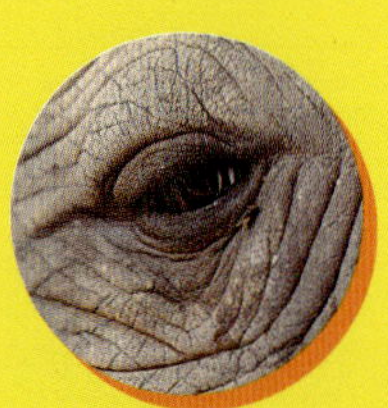 

nocturnal—active at night

ocelli—simple eyes with a single **lens** that can sense light and movement. One simple eye is an ocellus. Ocelli are found in insects and other **invertebrates**, such as worms.

peripheral vision—what is seen at the edges of vision without turning the head or moving the eyes

photoreceptors—cells that turn light into signals that can be understood by the brain

polarized light—**light waves** that vibrate at only one angle. Light that reflects off a pond or lake is polarized. Some animals can see polarized light.

predator—an animal that hunts other animals

prey—an animal that is hunted by other animals

pupil—the black opening at the center of the eye that gets larger and smaller to let in different amounts of light

retina—the area at the back of the eye that receives light and sends information to the brain as signals. See also **fovea**.

rod cells—the **photoreceptors** in **vertebrates** responsible for vision in low-light conditions

spectrum—the set of colors into which a beam of light can be separated: red, orange, yellow, green, blue, indigo, and violet. See also **wavelength**.

tapetum lucidum—a reflective layer behind the **retina** that reflects light back through the eye to boost night vision. It is found in many **nocturnal** animals.

trichromat—having three types of **cone cell** sensitive to three different **wavelengths** of light

ultraviolet light (UV)—light with a shorter **wavelength** than humans can see. Ultraviolet light is visible to many insects and birds.

vertebrate—an animal with a backbone, or spine. See also **invertebrate**.

wavelength—the distance between two peaks of **light waves**. Each color of the **spectrum** travels in waves of different lengths. Red has the longest wavelength, while violet has the shortest.

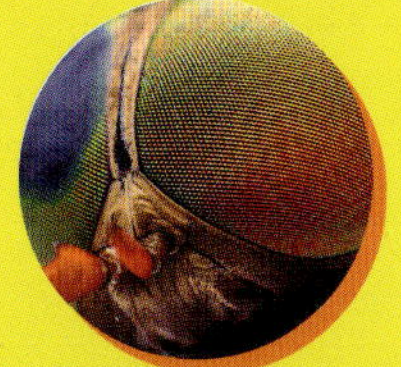

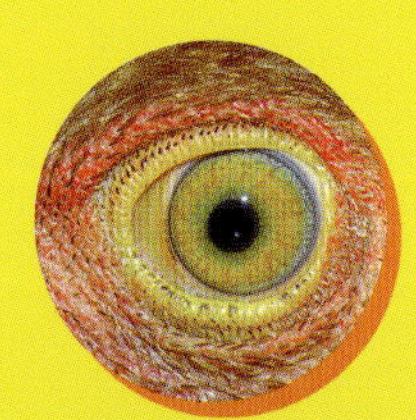

Written by Catherine Ard
Illustrated by Mat Edwards
Consultant: Professor Martin Stevens, University of Exeter

weldon**owen**

Published by Weldon Owen Children's Books
An imprint of Weldon Owen International, L.P.
A subsidiary of Insight Editions
PO Box 3088
San Rafael, CA 94912
www.insighteditions.com

Weldon Owen Children's Books
Senior Editor: Pauline Savage
Senior Designer: Clive Savage
Managing Editors: Toni Stemp and Mary Beth Garhart

Insight Editions
CEO: Raoul Goff
Senior Production Manager: Greg Steffen

ISBN: 979-8-88674-314-2

Manufactured in China by Insight Editions.
First printing, July 2025. RRD0725
10 9 8 7 6 5 4 3 2 1

Insight Editions, in association with Roots of Peace, will plant two trees for each tree used in the manufacturing of this book.